SandCastle™

First Sounds

Tracy and Trevor

Pam Scheunemann

Consulting Editor, Diane Craig, M.A./Reading Specialist

ABDO
Publishing Company

Published by ABDO Publishing Company, 4940 Viking Drive, Edina, Minnesota 55435.

Printed in the United States.

Credits
Edited by: Pam Price
Curriculum Coordinator: Nancy Tuminelly
Cover and Interior Design and Production: Mighty Media
Child Photography: Steven Wewerka, Wewerka Photography
Photo Credits: AbleStock, Photodisc

Library of Congress Cataloging-in-Publication Data

Scheunemann, Pam, 1955-
     Tracy and Trevor / Pam Scheunemann.
          p. cm. -- (First sounds)
     Includes index.
     ISBN 1-59679-200-0 (hardcover)
     ISBN 1-59679-201-9 (paperback)
        1. English language--Consonants--Juvenile literature. I. Title. II. Series.
     PE1159.S3435 2005
     428.1'3--dc22
                                                                                    2004059230

SandCastle™ books are created by a professional team of educators, reading specialists, and content developers around five essential components that include phonemic awareness, phonics, vocabulary, text comprehension, and fluency. All books are written, reviewed, and leveled for guided reading, early intervention reading, and Accelerated Reader® programs and designed for use in shared, guided, and independent reading and writing activities to support a balanced approach to literacy instruction.

Let Us Know

After reading the book, SandCastle would like you to tell us your stories about reading. What is your favorite page? Was there something hard that you needed help with? Share the ups and downs of learning to read. We want to hear from you! To get posted on the ABDO Publishing Company Web site, send us e-mail at:

sandcastle@abdopub.com

SandCastle Level: Emerging

tr

ABCDEFGH
IJKLMNOPQ
RSTUVWXYZ

abcdefgh
ijklmnopq
rstuvwxyz

3

Tracy

Trevor

truck

tree

tricycle

tray

train

The is blue.

The is big.

The is red.

Look at the .

Here is a .

Tracy sees a tree.

Trevor has a truck.

The tree is on the truck.

Which of these pictures begin with **tr**?

More words that begin with tr

tractor

trade

travel

tray

triangle

trick

trouble

true

About SandCastle™

A professional team of educators, reading specialists, and content developers created the SandCastle™ series to support young readers as they develop reading skills and strategies and increase their general knowledge. The SandCastle™ series has four levels that correspond to early literacy development in young children. The levels are provided to help teachers and parents select the appropriate books for young readers.

Emerging Readers
(no flags)

Beginning Readers
(1 flag)

Transitional Readers
(2 flags)

Fluent Readers
(3 flags)

These levels are meant only as a guide. All levels are subject to change.

To see a complete list of SandCastle™ books and other nonfiction titles from ABDO Publishing Company, visit www.abdopub.com or contact us at:
4940 Viking Drive, Edina, Minnesota 55435 • 1-800-800-1312 • fax: 1-952-831-1632